LE SPLEEN DE POUGHKEEPSIE

AKRON SERIES IN POETRY

Akron Series in Poetry

Mary Biddinger, Editor

Joshua Harmon, *Le Spleen de Poughkeepsie*
David Dodd Lee, *Orphan, Indiana*
Sarah Perrier, *Nothing Fatal*
Oliver de la Paz, *Requiem for the Orchard*
Rachel Dilworth, *The Wild Rose Asylum*
John Minczeski, *A Letter to Serafin*
John Gallaher, *Map of the Folded World*
Heather Derr-Smith, *The Bride Minaret*
William Greenway, *Everywhere at Once*
Brian Brodeur, *Other Latitudes*
Jeff Gundy, *Spoken among the Trees*
Alison Pelegrin, *Big Muddy River of Stars*
Roger Mitchell, *Half/Mask*
Ashley Capps, *Mistaking the Sea for Green Fields*
Beckian Fritz Goldberg, *The Book of Accident*
Clare Rossini, *Lingo*
Vern Rutsala, *How We Spent Our Time*
Kurt Brown, Meg Kearney, Donna Reis, Estha Weiner, eds., *Blues for Bill: A Tribute to William Matthews*
Sharmila Voorakkara, *Fire Wheel*
Dennis Hinrichsen, *Cage of Water*
Lynn Powell, *The Zones of Paradise*

Titles published since 2003.
For a complete listing of titles published in the series, go to www.uakron.edu/uapress/poetry

LE SPLEEN DE POUGHKEEPSIE

JOSHUA HARMON

The University of Akron Press
Akron, Ohio

All inquiries and permission requests should be addressed to the Publisher, the University of Akron Press, Akron, Ohio 44325-1703.

15 14 13 12 11 5 4 3 2 1

LIBRARY OF CONGRESS CATALOGING-IN-PUBLICATION DATA
Harmon, Joshua, 1971–
Le spleen de Poughkeepsie / Joshua Harmon. — 1st ed.
p. cm. — (Akron series in poetry)
ISBN 978-1-931968-93-5 (alk. paper) — ISBN 978-1-931968-92-8 (pbk. : alk. paper)
I. Title.
PS3608.A7485L4 2011
811'.6—DC22
2010047974

The paper used in this publication meets the minimum requirements of ANSI/NISO Z39.48–1992 (Permanence of Paper). ∞

Cover: *Animal Kingdom*, by Dan McCarthy, copyright © 2009. Used with permission. danmccarthy.org. Cover design: Amy Freels

Le Spleen de Poughkeepsie was designed and typeset by Amy Freels in Mrs. Eaves, with Hypatia Sans display. *Le Spleen de Poughkeepsie* was printed on sixty-pound natural and bound by BookMasters of Ashland, Ohio.

ACKNOWLEDGMENTS

Some of these poems were first published, sometimes in different forms, in *Absent*, *Agni*, *Colorado Review*, *Copper Nickel*, *Massachusetts Review*, *Mid-American Review*, *New South*, *The Offending Adam*, *Sentence: A Journal of Prose Poetics*, *Typo*, and *Volt*.

Some of these poems also first appeared in the chapbook *The Poughkeepsiad* (The Greying Ghost Press).

Many thanks to these friends for their help with this book: Paige Ackerson-Kiely, Geoff Bouvier, Karin Gottshall, Josh Russell, Allison Titus, and Andrew Zawacki. Thanks to G. C. Waldrep, Carl Annarummo, and the inexhaustible Mary Biddinger. Deepest thanks to Sarah Goldstein.

"The Poughkeepsiad" is dedicated to Hua Hsu.

"[What are the pitfalls…]" is dedicated to Paige Ackerson-Kiely.

The initial versions of "Two Pastorals (II)" were written in the company of Andy Axel, Carolyn Bergonzo, Kyle Holter, Brian Kim, and Danielle Unger—as well as the spirit of Max Lewin—and are dedicated to them.

To the flâneurs of College Avenue, with thanks for the whisky and sympathy: Heesok, Carrie, Michael, Ann, Hua, Paul, Amitava, Halimah, Larissa, Jake, and, as ever, Sarah—

Contents

J'omets la description du taudis…

—Charles Baudelaire,
Le Spleen de Paris

TWO PASTORALS

The automatic garage-door opener
lifts on a prospect of Poughkeepsie:
row of parked cars along curb, man
leaf-blowing each falling leaf,
sumac growing beneath the overpass:
if you're not part of the problem,
you're part of the lengthening
tragedy: we see all the others
slipped into the bright shapes of endeavor,
imprints snow slowly fills, but the stray
detours and workarounds of the secret
city inside the more obvious one
elude our plundered adornments
and church-bell quarter-hours:
on the outskirts of the absurd
attention to the material life,
of course the factories are empty
and the train line overgrown,
and the everyday fills the ravine
beside the highway: the passive voice
speaks on our winds and in the humming
of our truck tires, the delicacy
of Saturday-night videophoning
and bonfires across the valley
in woods past their peak

To Shop-Vac the sidestreet
of one's grass clippings
is to say I am dispossessed
of a deeper fortitude
with which I might lose
track of the beam or the bank
supporting the idea
of deliverance from myself
and other, similar errors:
later, the cruiser spotlights
semi-suburban houses,
those dark alleys emptied
but for early woodsmoke and diesel
fumes paid on or before
this inescapable duty resolved
shortfalls in neighborliness,
and the engine running all night
inside a garage does not kill
the murderous rage you feel:
the working life peaces out
and declares its independence

THE POUGHKEEPSIAD

I cannot disappear from circumstances
where I'd like to find myself least

—Laynie Browne,
Daily Sonnets

Behind the pines, the proof of experience
where juncos lift and disperse, the capacity
in branches, and all the repetitions in sound
and movement of the spirits animating a vast snarl
of plastic sheeting slung through the upper
canopy of an oak: and in the girl who didn't
brush her hair this morning, and the parking lot
where the windows of a rust-blossomed SUV
are greased with the breath of the man passed out
inside it: the woman at the bagel shop speaks
impulses of wiring and transistors, and another
woman carries a neat plastic bag wrapping dogshit: three
sleepy media theorists on work-study at the call center forget
themselves: an autistic rain stutters over Poughkeepsie,
glazing concrete seams and scuffed plexiglass,
the previously held reality of the day labor
division, and the young couple holding hands
on a dented guardrail, and from such misinterpretations
red and white lights blur out of acquiescence, a fury
of notional data like the fenced-off
pile of rain-slicked brick and cracked
moldings, or bright whorls of leaves blown down
the valley: the precariously possible
gifts of life: blood on a billboard, and how
to deal with loss, the radical idea that the sky is white:
the sky is pink over a block of derelict homes in the city
where I can't look at you alone: at the bodega
across the street, a scratch ticket gets rubbed out
like everything invisibly escaping: perp face-down
on the sidewalk still entangled in missing
twelve-speed, perps running barefoot
through an orchard, sleeping bags
left unrolled in crushed grass: or the newspaper

version: battered storm door, booklet
of paper matches and talismanic prerequisites,
flea-market snapshots curling in a drawer:
while her six-year-old
daughter sleeps in the next room, shadows
of birds course past sheer curtains: and wind
presses newsprint against the chain-link
around the schoolyard where, across a muddy
left field, small children chase smaller children:
in this context a benign word's best practices achieve
preferred status, like the idling gypsy cab
when the train returns along the river—five
dollars takes you anywhere in this town
except out of it: the misplaced sentimentality
of it all finds no-brainers embedded in a translation
of spraypainted brick into pursuits
that enhance the burden for evangelism:
raindrops pinned on the black cherry's thorns, talk
radio voice, low-carbohydrate bread eaten
to fill a need less desperate than that of the skunk
trapped beside the Jersey barrier,
but only the wind makes me cry, its inhumane
tongue and vagabond rhythms cross-faded
into a slippery use of the second person: nothing
we say exists beyond involuntary
separations: on the bus, a man can't stop touching
the loose flap of Band-Aid on his thumb,
a re-prioritized friendship in 8-bit graphics: encryption
is a metaphor for what's wrong with the city
where I can't look at you right now: someone has lost
a canvas tote, and someone has lost a rabbit-fur glove
and an understanding of Spanish that might
prove helpful, and someone has lost a small white dog

last seen running down Hooker Ave., and someone
has abandoned pretense, another drained bottle
in crumpled brown bag: please call
if found: "we find ourselves plagued by unimaginable
circumstances," and the laryngitic voice speaks
of preludes, the ornaments and spires of the horizon
we wear out with watching: a man pushes a double
stroller toward the checkout counter, child too old
to be pushed in one half, eighteen-beer box of Budweiser
in the other—"Thanks, man"—and the woman
behind him shifts a dozen bags of candy
in her arms: another man steers a wire cart
loaded with the music of aluminum
cans, and this is only one reason why
no one in Poughkeepsie wants
to take harp lessons at the house on the private
drive: the metronomic force of wood-splitting
multiplies in floodlit backyards, off garage and fence
and jacked-up car, wheelless and windowless
in whatever apparent weather suggests it's going
to get colder: and it gets colder: at 6 AM,
a man outside the bakery breathes curls and
wisps, hands clamped in his armpits, cursing:
the weather that makes knuckles bleed, that
upholsters certitude: and the single-engine
airplane that appears to descend
through dun winter sky into wind
-rattled phragmites, when does it return:
thrift-store imperative: bearded man
in baseball cap, woman standing over him,
her mascara-tinted tears more than we figured on
when down the road the afternoon sermon is successful
soul-winning: but there are no souls to be rummaged

from leaf-scattered slopes, from rusted rebar poking through
crumbling concrete: the vagaries of need all work
toward some other formula, a vodka-and-soda
lifestyle set down amid old architectures,
the repetitions insistence scans for illegible
memories in a gas station sign's mismatched numerals:
low-res flurries under streetlights'
sodium blush, and what's accomplished
by handheld footage, like the pebbled texture
of styrofoam coffee cup held by the woman
looking out duct-taped plate glass at you looking
in as you pass: the doorway another woman
ducks into to fix a flame to the end
of a cigarette like all the misunderstood pleasures
of color, and the furnace that quits one cold
morning over an out-of-place wire, a $120 wire:
but telephone lines string us along
the extant daydreams of the man ironing
a pair of trousers and wandering some greener
world: the noise of beauty,
noise of the bullet the cop blasts into the heart
of the traffic-struck doe kicking limply
beside the road, broken stalks
and broken legs in headlights now busted:
a woman wants to know which Bordeaux
to bring to dinner, or how frayed and ethereal
credit card digits are magnified by
the restlessness of short-handed theorems, so we
try to rescue declaration from its wilderness self:
colder still, and flannel shirts and herbal remedies
fail us: at the edges of the yard, beyond the pines,
beyond the privacy fence, beyond this city's broken
nose, beyond what sound shapes into another used-up

opinion: work not getting done, acts of imagining
aftermath, trail of chicken bones
along the street, and a lift home, white-noise
machine to obliterate the Poughkeepsie night:
immigrant raid at the hair salon, peeled
-back foil blister pack on windowsill, hurtful
winter sun unread by men shifting weight
from foot to foot beside a strip of rental-car pennants
where they wait for a ride to install drywall, silent
TV screen gone over to violent
snow, all the last thoughts from a one-bedroom
in the frigid north:
after the creosote ignites in the chimney
and roof timbers blacken and collapse, the people
with bare heads and bare arms gathered in the street
under the splendor of fire-truck lights watch
their breath lift and disperse in parched arctic
air with the roiling yellow smoke
of plastic toys and composition shingles, and a salt truck
scatters calcium chloride on the rippled ice
from hose-spills: later, a hazy piece of moon
backlights the house in pale blue:
the lack of affect in an oversized raccoon
examining the ruin all the protection we thought
we needed: still, I can't look with your cartographic
scrutiny at the porch light shining in daytime
when the geezer baffled by the tiny tattered flag
he flies from his radio antenna returns
to his driveway, thinking of political loyalties,
an invitation to retire from seemingly
meaningful coincidences, or how to make
a distinction about why something was let go:
another boombox sermon, and imaginary

municipalities of strip mall treelines get knocked over
with a front-end loader: but a diminishment
of light scrolls upward
like a screen flickering from overload or vast
swirls of starlings, errant e-mails caught in
a bramble of downed wires:
and the girl hiding beneath her bed for hours
thinks it's going to end
but it never ends:
in the T.J. Maxx plaza there is a new tenant,
and in the sunlit parking lot the brilliant
windshields of cars whelm
the occupants of a Honda as the traffic-flow
analyst waits at a four-way stop
and considers his next move:
"My life now is very economical"

TABLEAUX POUGHKEEPSIENS

I lived in one place
and then I lived

in another until I came
to Poughkeepsie:

such comic historicizing,
like sweeping up nineteenth

-century dusts and the
twenty-first-century

cigarette that's fallen
from behind someone's ear,

or a spray of class C
pyrotechnics captured

in digital pixels from a clearing
in sparse woods, seems less

a misreading of the social text
than a chastisement of devotion

to our deleted shadows

Asbestos in carpet glue, beige linoleum in bedroom and living room, hallway and kitchen: the thinnest wisps of whatever boredom burns itself into, an insufferable inching toward wreckage. The man with a hand in your drawers is only checking for mice. The porch light's gone, the door thrown open, and a dice game binds the ghostlier commodities to blown-out tires and traffic tickets, the smallest conveniences handed over a counter. A simplism: I have a lawnmower if you have money. A boy watching over the lip of his particular attachments: mediocre pen pal in the instrumental version. A mercy killing: the wall-to-wall. Deer step softly to the back window to receive all our coveted inadequacies. The estranged husband falls asleep in an armchair amid afternoon sun and taped cardboard boxes, then wakes to turn in for the night. All night, the train. And trees branch over the road in the precise shape of the absence of a truck's right-angled trailer: so many pre-existing contentions.

A pole saw can reach far enough one doesn't need a bucket truck to clear some sky. We're cutting down our half of the tree, you can do what you like with yours. I'm exhausted raking orange needles and clearing dead leaves from my gutters, and anyway imagine summer sun ablaze on aluminum siding, or tracing the low winter sun's arc all the way home, chimneys and telephone poles, long-disconnected television aerials weeping rusty smears on shingles, wind undoing old birds' nests. All afternoon, a handheld circular saw slices wood pallets to fit a stove's mouth. A pause goes on and on, more vacant than not, but ghosts do not hang from the birches of Christians who carve crosses into the faces of hollowed pumpkins encoded with incomplete legends. The children pile like puppies before the woodstove's banked flames and curl themselves to sleep. Can we imagine another world? Pity keeps it going.

Cusp of July and August:
subtlety's landscape of westward

decline, mountains bottoming out
in brick river-towns: the digital

thermometer registers more than we can
feel, the hyper logic of resale:

doe lifts hoof from hosta-bed,
a suburban orchestration: clattering

dice and dusk's late sepia, urgency
of compressed air driving nails

under hard disk clouds' silent quotations,
austere as hand-washed linens

Thin ribbons of cloud and half a ruinous moon
in an afternoon sky: meager sun gilds asphalt

briefly and slides out of sight as the furnace
kicks on again: in the tumult of equivalences

between split log and smoke, margin and note,
my knowledge unbraids itself from freed

finitudes: and whatever sense of the possible
the afternoon offers vanishes in a lethal twilight

broken by a single steeple, an abandoned
railway bridge spanning here and there, value

and use, the shapes this city assumes

Broken glass in the shape of
standing still on a side

porch: but Poughkeepsie

has the same shape
as an agonized self

-awareness: fingertips

against wall-shadow,
girl smoking in the kitchen

with the dishwashing crew,

narrative flukes like holding
a sign beside the divided

highway for the liquidation

sale: everything discounted:
if history has been

the consummation of keep

-sakes and solitude,
proficiencies in consent

and other remaindered

eventualities, the double
garage the ailanthus grows

through grows historical:

interpretation rusts
to depict the housekeeping

motel with riverview,

two-week stay's currency of
handwritten diaries,

where an hour past checkout

the landlord collects
the television tipped into

weeds by the back door

The undercity rivers beneath cast
-iron covers: passage we know

only when set loose on windy
avenues ourselves: a world of nouns

in leaf-debris carried curbside
and the blunt animus of hammers

on vinyl machined into clapboards:
a confident inability to focus:

or a graph upon worm-eaten vine
leaves addled on frost-dead

stalks: progress's ordinary commerce
gets stranded in this town's vacancies

and intervening scraps: so noise
becomes intently irregular, skittering

windwardly amid the working
class shrubberies and filtering

maple leaves of a garage-sale
economy: the non-negotiable

vocal inflections and muttered
curses of father and son

rebuilding the house they
crowbarred for kindling last year

Does it help that the evening no
longer smells of smoke? That hammer-blows
have quieted? I'm asking you, moon,
not the seventy-foot silver maple:

brittle limbs and unrotted trunk piece
-meal for morning's front-end loader, loan
of remote-controlled stump-grinder: slow
bleed of boredom that won't cripple:

so do you keep a lossy secret
in which you are not erased, not a point
to attach a scaffold in front
of, or mangle the oncoming winter:

trying to intuit survival by
its effects instead of its causes

Crow-scatter engraves evening, wings beating
westward: sometimes things get lost between us

In a geography of service drives and sumac
hedges, these brick stacks no longer exhaust

us, but the old unpronounceable molecules
remain in the worn-away grass

of a side-yard's sewer line like lesser angels
exist in the canes of an English rose

trained from Hudson alluvium
through a wire fence: and the visual

space of the most constrained sky
redistributing digital winds amid

an awkward civilian truce advances
its own agenda: the ravished heresies

of the unspoken, a house we should not
have occupied, the evasions of the trees

Deer cross against the lights
of future-tense cars: an idea

of elsewhere as they run
into backyard tomato gardens:

dusk, and deer appear
at ditch brush edges: deer

appear to have lost themselves
in what I will not help you

understand: the forgotten
familiar wakes me, and kids

ruin the sketch of telephone
wires, the floodlight

that freezes deer where they stand,
lawn ornaments beside birdfeeder

and plaster urn: fringe friend
at a costume party, how

is it that other people
experience me the way

boys bang bicycles against rocks
down power line washouts?

A number are wounded,
and refuse to go back.

An inquiry into more forlorn subjects neglects unsolvable winter's photocopied twilight. Well, review your own company: whining dog, mice scrabbling laths, fugitive self-interest, reheated coffee, decades of dust in radiator fins: and three boys trundling a dead car down the alley want to be included, too. A kick-ass attentiveness bunny-hops the curb and tires of chronology: once there were reasons in the caliber of resentments. The infrared flyover will reveal different family groups otherwise invisible in dark trees, a footnote to be sold at a loss. I feel kind of blessed not to be around you.

The provisional, the mostly blank implied in a twenty-year-old space heater with fraying cord: even the miniscule changes since our last visit can engage our wandering eyes. We get off on an hourly rate as unaccountable in evening as the scent of cigarettes in still air. A hubcap rattles off a van, a housefly troubles a window painted shut, and the perpendicular life whistles its way home. So many short streets ending in guardrails. Perched on a lightpole, a crow cease-fires the self-effacing sunset. If we could count all the pennies in the till. If we could unexpect. If we could blunt our cartoon destinies. If the hardest-to-please neighbor could stuff a drawer with all her swept-up dusts and solitary errands.

The disheartened public
space arranges what you get

away with and what you thought
you knew: the knowledge

of door-to-door pamphleteers,
or the schoolteacher arriving

at a late regard for wine
by the glass and his own minimal

importance: if you break the rules
then you deserve the consistencies:

the wide spread of scattershot
can rip your ribs open

with a double blast: the other
forms this platitude takes

do not have a right to be
here when not working,

as in, "Can we just get rid of
Poughkeepsie little by little?"

The quiet streets of meth
dispensaries closed

for the holiday
weekend: blossom

of razorwire,
and barbed hooks

of autumn-dried briers
it encloses: outfit

intelligence with such
defenses, one

-two combo enough
is enough that need

not avert its spectacled
gaze from motion

-sensitive garage lights,
from the unadorned

fluctuations of
morning TV:

Can new tedium distract one
from tedium that already exists

in smoke-colored branches against smoke
-colored skies and the mumble of traffic

and voices, or is the retreat ambushed?
The crux of small words: folding

chair seats changing hands without a vote,
blinds never raised at the house

across the street, and we forget
that our neighbors have died or been

handcuffed: but in a slight portrait
of mediocrity and boredom, the artist

has neglected a signature: the
recurring optimism of sycamores

and rhododendrons as sirens wake us up
again and the inner landscape reboots itself

Bare-branched maples, brush
-stroked November noon
sky fading as far as Poughkeepsie
can dream: browned-out
thicket and pines' older
music, frost-curled frond, blanched

seed husk split to ribbed
beige, aster, hawkweed, stiff
chicory stalk, mullein, golden
-crowned pileups, feathered
twigs under milky sun,
spar and scrag...

The friskiest winds return:
yes, Poughkeepsie's occasion
-al disheveled beauty

Not one, but dozens of solitary dandelions sparsely studding the vivid green grass of the leach field this near-freezing November afternoon.

To build a life from happy accidents
of scrap metal and dumb luck's dumber

purpose, twin bereavements in flannel
shirts and hand-me-down jeans: a sense

of what's been erased: pageant of veterans
with hunting knives and gas cans, menthol

mouths and kids in their underwear on
the front steps: not everyone can afford

such illuminating thoughts: but we can
take into our home the daughter

of the woman who killed her mother
and teach her interstitial faith,

rest-stop travel and a river's surface
noise, end-timed desire: how to bless

the day, how to survive Poughkeepsie
winters: inelegant shorthand of canned soups

and plastic-sheeted windows hair
-dryered smooth, the tampered data

of what a small girl knows

Slice of hillside
woods should

-ering a ballfield,
between vinyl

-clad American four
-square and lowlier

ranch, cast-iron vent
pipes thicket-thick:

broken trees and trio
of horizontal

wires, tire-flattened
cat carcass spook

-ing unsidewalked road
-side a season until grass

overtakes itself and greens
again: the thinnest

gravestones tilt beneath
condominium oaks

We shoot everything you want to
remember: two rusty bikes

chained to lamppost, metal mesh
hung from hoops at frost-heaved court:

feng shui cannot redeem
the elaborate hoax of care

taken in this town's furniture,
nor a cassette capture its granular

realities: why do I
complain? You said, "Be cool."

Still and slate-dark by four-thirty
at the plexiglass bus shelter:
the season for giving
up on the diminishments and giving
nothing away, forgiving no one
for the experiences we left home for

I slept on a varnished oak floor. I slept on scar tissue and sourced sympathies. I slept with the smallest bottle of whisky the liquor store sold, slept through gruesome histories of endurance like an eyelash stuck to a cheek. I wanted to inspect the most dissolute voltages. The residue of a holograph. My property was a girdling root, but the desolation was real.

To be freed from the burden
of being no more important

than anyone else: neck
tattoo and half-ton,

recuperated history like
last night's leftovers

on the sidewalk, meter
reader stuck in the mirror

phase beside the laundromat's
gentle clang and fragrances:

the ritual mourners of Poughkeepsie
find the rock-salt path home

The house shudders in wind
like living with my girlfriend

for the first time:

we perish quickly,
but not quickly

enough for those who would

replace us with a sense
of untold relief

overlooked in the blurred

drone of morning:
imagine the safe return

of perplexment as the six-car

train rumbles by: if I stand in
the middle of the street long

enough, it will come to me:

Milkweed and broken sink,
stand of browned goldenrod,

blitz of rust-orange blow
-down: yes, dear twilight, I

like to be alone with
scents of sill-dust and gasoline

pump handles: a controlled
excess historically

received with the clank
and smudge of defunct

industry: wind at a window:
where is that music your letter

spoke of: the civilizing
purpose of a physical place

we can return to
like collecting plastic

bottles from a hilltop
amid grassy footsteps

and unhappy prospects,
some textual weeping

to suggest a frozen pond's
regional reality,

or syntax's late
abandonment: the best

source of everyday value
as the rains blow in

Only the immeasurable
holes machines make

in lawful ground, last
leaf-lace, light of flat

screen colors left: a stubborn
magnitude like a hungry

boy's elusiveness
to the world: palm prints

on sliding glass
door braced with dowel,

concrete balcony beyond,
enforced apology and

private sense of backlit clouds:
I would give anything:

Poor little Poughkeepsie,
alone without delusions,

as if two blocks of wood
were knocked together:

already, snow in the hills
and two refrigerator

shelves given over
to sideways bottles of beer:

it's a dick move, the endearing
way you forget your wallet

for five percent off night
at the grocery store: why

don't the kids aiming rocks
at plastic cups floating in the pond

understand the borders
of reconstructed grace:

the dog lifts its paw
and refuses to walk,

a heads-up for those adrift
at a drive-thru, or huffing

hairspray in the kitchen
and nodding off

to car alarms and turbulent
sparrow-song like compressed

files: nightfall's inevitable
murmurs gone for days now

What are the pitfalls you have come to know intimately? Which wind-drifted ashes will you claim as your own? What are the odds of a chainsaw moaning in the trunk of an ice-decapitated pine? I can still fathom the recurring mentions of a Toyota wobbling past on a donut, the public telephone beside the courthouse steps, the pieces of experience out in the vastness, or the ecstatic desire for soccer-field solitude, but not the mattresses chucked in the backyard dumpster, or the mattresses wedged into the bed of a pickup, or the pink tufts of insulation blown across trampled grass, or all the other absentminded particulars of ruin. Rain performs sorceries of dissolution. Rain-slashes on a window. Rain scaffolding a sky. Rain pixellates the afternoon.

The quivering powerlines could be a word. A dry cleaning bag's thin sheen on a fence could adorn a nostalgia, the same nostalgia I've had for years. What future's not frightening? Blue jay in bluer sky: I was the thinnest sock on a February afternoon. I was a younger sister's understanding of what cushions remorse. An unpatrolled motive. An abbreviated escort home. A monotone thicket's stiff gray on gray on mingled gray graffitis the curves of a devotion untelling itself as it goes.

I'm trying to whittle this skyline down to something more manageable, the skinny smoke of a campfire instead of all the slivers of distant trees and towers clanging against the grayness. But the wonders of mending have their own lethargy, and the snow's been down long enough to have trouble accounting for that: a cloudier evening.

The view from basement
windows through yellow
grasses brittle between
paving squares: sparrows
light from minor arcs and
the earth's curve offers me
smokestacks: the splice
where church-bell peals
and appeals are joined
to phrases like this one:
sock holes and test patterns,
the concepts a shovel's worked
over when the parents
aren't home, a body bound
to a place of declining
balances and a sycamore's
displacements: they are
rebuilding the city
from a hatchback filled
with day-old loaves and all
the appropriate resentments:
a lesson in looking good
with a cigarette and magnifying
one's own restlessness,
fashions in felt-tipped pen:
the redneck hegemon in
costume dramas beside
the warehouse's dirty snowpiles:
and our own kingdom
goes, unaccountably

Seed-flecked snow
and glacial night, curves

of scraped road: misgivings
athwart a guardrail, blue

-black hour: we choose
the courtesy of suffering

our friends' exile to
the men's room's engaging

tracts, a concrete life
inhabiting city spirits,

the polymered drift
of particulate winds,

a salted river: blinding ice
and trees, snow rags

and sky's rags as, silvered,
the circle's clipped:

birches break under
ice's weight and that

of their own branches:
the full range of unspanned

spaces in view, a single
staked poplar: a wake

for understanding
the throes of subtlety,

the higher places of belief
and unused light

It's cinematic, the blank billboard at the edge of the woodlot: available. The houses are available, and an ersatz drunkenness is available, and a little snow completes the night. A plow blade chips away at a forfeited afterlife. The soul uploads winter on a dial-up line and awaits affirmation. Spruce boughs bend against primitive roof, and as I start to forget the legal loudness of a muffler on a truck painted with red and yellow flames, an uncontrollable restraint stretches itself between cold sheets and grinds its teeth for hours. Sparks from a jumper cable. Speech bubble filled with black marks. The way moonlight stains snow that's thawed and re-frozen so many times calls my bluff. The wind still says "As if..."

The iciest particulars: I was exhausted from waking up. A view can be achieved with some clearing of hardwired obligations. The scraped-together snow still will not melt in the parking lot everyone uses to miss the light, though wide puddles obscure the potholes. And on the first warm day, the downy woodpecker that outlasted winter on suet cakes brains itself on a window's reflection: the intimacies with strangers just another capacity for going astray. I'm hesitating over interruptions, the unending opportunities in long-haul caregiving, and all the overlooked implements of diversification, but in DelForno's deli, the talk is of absent ghosts and rainy-day luminaries. "All I do is push off," says the man in the bloodstained apron. The camera pans up to the sky above the apartment stack to track a swing of pigeons, but, in the foreground, millennial sunlight falls on the faces of nineteenth-century houses with security bars over their windows. Admission requires no more than a knack for speaking the language, but no one comes here out of a sense of resignation.

A parking
-lot seagull
blown up
-river
and the French
fry wrapper
it chokes down:
end-of-winter,
sand-strewn
pavement, sell
me some
-thing better

As blackened snow retreats from curb and gutter, signs of color in leaf litter: blue of Pepsi can, yellow of winter aconite. In the road, crows unravel the intestines of a pulped squirrel. The jagged semi-windows of the Luckey-Platt building reflect a semi-sunset. Good Friday, and Christian boys, toothmarks on their arms, wrestle in a muddy side yard.

The perilous optic, 3 AM in the back of an American sedan: ninety percent chance of fickle indifference—one thing, infinite things, wherever untroubled smoke rises from a restaurant's exhaust fan with no room for sentimentality, wherever the suburban motorcade roams: places we may have attempted, or felt: a literal denotation of the fact that a thing *is* itself is unnecessary, but absurder visions anoint implosions of what happened, late one night in Poughkeepsie, on the way home: because fragmentation doesn't indicate failure, only its possibility, a noisy nothingness: I am inundated: a desiccated self's elopements: and spring's sidestreet leaf tunnels, electrically diffuse: order of brisk dawns aside more eager sorrows and engine-block strivings: it rains on skinny forsythia, on peeling porch steps, on all the misappellations of thrift: no room for an audience to drive home safely:

O springtime foliage! This city's last slate rooftops refute the Hudson's sluggish empathies. Our unowned, our best-loved: whisky-with-water, dogshelter photo, temporary toilet in gravel lot, absolute belief in the readymade: a place no longer foreign. And a pattern language in weather's cheat codes. Two flip-flops dropped in pollen-rimmed puddle: we've received offers, but none worth taking. Where else might we find the most beautifully tuned car alarm? Where else the most wayward attachment still on speaking terms with inauthentic brick? The zoning laws of suitcase and hide-a-way bed can be counted some other audition of annulment. Headlights strobe on plaster ceiling. No use rereading the sense of extravagantly endless days.

The elegance of an only focus, a trance
of under-indulgence: juvenilia in a glass

ashtray atop the scuffed dresser: a wash
costs $2.75 more than the smell of dusty

streets during the thundershower, a form
of beauty nobody realized was beautiful:

and the janitor greets night at the back
door: what do I care about diction,

or a pine tree wearing a spraypainted cross,
a feral kitten licking coconut milk

cans left unrinsed in the recycling bin,
some citizen's idea of myth, the boys outside

the 7-Eleven who stand away from a truth
about the flimsiness of captivities

Children wire stuffed
animals and plastic flowers

to a fence, chalk numbered
squares on the sidewalk:

a broken broom handle and an un-
asked question, the point at the crown

of a hoodie drawn tight:
the walls are thin and the gate

squeaks, and the doorknob came off
in her hand: thought provoking

a louder radio, tuned to
the static of some stadium

crowd: so hearsay keeps it
real behind plywood windows

while an upstairs light goes out,
mantra of midsummer

streets: ownership
of this afternoon

suppressed by arterial traffic
trusting what it knows

Amid the last sentences of rusting
public sculptures in early-hours fog,

everything disorganizes itself
the way a ground-floor window left

open overnight does justice to
this city: the numbers suggest that

the woman watching three generations
of automobiles sliding along the street

and the crisis in a microsuede couch
with a hand-lettered sign reading "bedbugs"

resents her inevitabilities less than
the man who can continue only by turning away

from the grievances he marries to a lost
argument like noise decays in empty space:

slowly: all the intolerable surfaces, but still
I could stare out her window all day

The greatest poverty is not to live
in Poughkeepsie, to wear a fleece
blanket against a diner's air
-conditioning, to ride a motorcycle
shirtlessly and helmetlessly along
a sidewalk beneath blighted maples:
how long till you succumb
to the accidental nature
of nature, your own nature, spaces
to fill in later: a naked torso
over an engine, a folk song of fire
escapes and bottlecaps: you can't live here
and I can't leave, but you can
come down for a weekend
of inaccurate impulses
amid an overperfumed mall's
bodily distortions, the rough housing
of foggy suburbs and the mutually
assured ruin of every qualified sense

The absent tenant's electricity is shut off for nonpayment, and for two July weeks the twelve-pound turkey in the freezer thaws. Fluttering curtains, half-turned head, window lit with a single bulb: anyone can tell this story, but what can you say to the relentless demented music of an ice cream truck? To a cardboard box cabin in the woods behind the dumpsters where deer forage, or a coatimundi caged by chicken wire in a basement? The men, encircled, will not lay down their chainsaws, so the boys and girls sharing a bed are sent away. The Mayor of Spoor Avenue turns down his hearing aid, but through polarized bifocals scowls at the inviolate discipline of a summer school bus, or the board of trade negotiating a key drop at the yellow house. A memoir of disintegration: "We only drink the bible water." So many garages for rent, but a tarp stretched over the bed of the pickup truck will hold off the rain a while longer. From a nest inside the illuminated O on a strip mall's façade, a starling watches too.

HOOKER AVENUE SERENADE

An aluminum box fan in a window
and rain's ruckle in the leaves:
Poughkeepsie during the reign
of summer's anonymity:
a telegraphic tangent
as if the disbursement would take
less time than whatever backyard
insurrection we see ourselves
fighting: the urban developmentally
disabled shoot hoops off
the absence of a twelve-hour
workday and elaborate reprisals
against a worn gear: we may
memorize the sounds of cars,
the scent of scalded coffee
in a paper cup, the provisional
evening's offhand weather and
the decadent position of picket
-fence espionage, the urge,
the reason: it's all
embarrassing, a historical
fiction, like the corona
of a streetlight in an abiding haze,
or forty-one hundredths
of an acre: will build to suit
the most primitive needs:
but in the documentary
of fulfillment, the arcana of
the inner lives in the inner city
in our keeping annul emotional
reactions to rustproofed circumstances,
as when the band kicks into an uptempo
4/4 inside the parked car

where a man sits, one door slung ajar
and a post-surgical leg extended
like the persistent concussions
of masculinity: it is context,
not event: your world and your
pronoun, the index of your company
and the discordances of things unframed:
the reification of leisure and the dead
moths blown in from a windowsill
'cause that's the way thunderstorms roll
down from the hills to summer's
squandered extenuations: I inhabit
outcomes in order to disappoint
myself with the traces
of a single diminishment, like
the fourteen-year-old girl from down
the street who aims a flashlight
through my mail slot and asks me
to call the police: or the other
girl in the video walking
quietly along a brick sidewalk
with a plastic bag caught on her foot
until the camera loses her
around a corner: but the still
lives abolish themselves
in our unstructured privacies
when all the young girls worry
about the restoration
of peer groups in the confines
left by decency and need:
up through another night,
a rabbity boredom remains
in the purifying force of a limited

vocabulary grafted to a delay
that shadows darker moments
under rain-rosaried power
lines: under the most democratic
rain: the most diligent rain:
up through the night,
the rituals and conditions
call in sick to spend earliest
morning revisiting the fugitive appeals
of retouched and worthless grief,
the crookedest lines apparent
in an arbitrary realism:
like a dream of more correct uses
for loose facts: we own what we do
in between the workings of the work
and the power of two cameras
on the tallest buildings in a small city:
up all night, rewinding the tape-spliced beats
of moth wings on a screen
flecked with rain: and how do I fit in
-to the vision of the young woman
I saw, arms scrolled with ink,
chemical hair, steering her
wheelchair outside the chain
-linked basketball court's three-on-three:
the attention to another body's
elements, the most spectacular
passages: and the usual methods
of news-gathering, such as seven
satellite dishes bolted to asbestos
shingles, or the observer's
unmeasured position by a window:
a blinking amber half

a mile away that no one
witnesses, a landmark we get
so far from home: and rain: “I’m like
the king of a rainy country”: but
even the verdant gardens
begin to rot: we live so near the thorough
-fare’s finite comforts, the last
legitimate wreckage: and my
memory is made of brick and concrete

RECESSIVE VARIATIONS

I.

Green spikes grow
from rain
-gutters and leaves:
phoneme
of maul and wedge,
violence of things
unconnected
connected: phone me,
month of dusks
and hooked sun
-flower heads seed
-heavy, goldfinched: a
single gesture
like a preference
for grass
fires and sleeping
on your belly,
for newsprint
glyphs on your
unmooned fingers,
the momentary
erased by the galvanized
reconstructions
of a scoured
city scorned
by rubble: and shadows
respond to rain
on the river
sequestering push
-pin maps and gridded in
-cantations of an
unarrayed din:

perforated roof-light
where green spikes
inherit a bracket
of hands
-on lessons yearning
for bandwidth: scraps
and a home's easy tilt,
a rafter's plastic
-sheeted certainty
immolated with,
undercast with
the makeshift
and the make-workings
of a willing mind,
scrawls unstunted
like afternoon
adheres to you:
one photo-booth
leftover one day-old
marriage one scope
of seeing stints
in warehoused climates,
power grid slurs
of response and debrised
gravities, boxed
and unused
to interlockings
of source and clatter,
cast-off copybooks:
erratic insects
trafficking in trees'
late summer self
-enunciations:

and water
weeps from air
-conditioner
spouts: thumbprint
of cloud and thumbprint
in plaster, clotheslines
of cricket-skirmished
script, decomposable
gray leaves
to which fragility
adds its color,
stranded, undivided:
residuals stammer
a paragraph's grit

II.

Like the horizon
-tal line, the coupon
won't scan
and the line
grows long
at the register:
slow piano
music of traffic,
garbage cans
dragged curbside
to sunlight's last
orange transcriptions
of horizon
and clearest sky:
size 11 footprints
in concrete, one
watered, all
blurred: a last word
a pictogram
a property line
seen through narrowed
blinds: and renewal
proceeds from the effects
of historic
cloud bequests and
telepathic improv:
a wall stripped
to studs, a house
husked to studs
and joists, offset
frame, anecdote
of hearth and weather

we desire more
than the boy with
chisel and hammer
who imitates the space
where you left off:
early-hours birdsong
from the alley behind
the garage: dim
diminutives of
distance against
brick specifics
and taillight thinking,
sheet-metal mornings:
broken antenna
voiceless the way
speech bubbles
forth from a drain
-pipe in the ditch
below the park:
nonstop:

FOR THE POUGHKEEPSIE DEAD

I.

The ice caps have melted
and scribed in asphalt

and the grime of panel
trucks directives to love

or be loved, the favorite song
at the college where a full

moon rises over the golf course
and empty beer cans

rattle on gravel: a delayed
pithiness like flaking aluminum

siding sunlit to reflect
another shopping-cart

journey: a guttering
candle and awkward

limp home to haunt an
unfathomed future of Norway

maples and plastic sheds:
the last thing I noticed

in the noise surrounding
the local watering hole,

the polyester night sky
that moves its long tail

as if dreaming in the wake
of passing trucks along

blacktop where you should never
will a change so near the end

II.

In order to live, to find
your way among broken streets

or the shapes of impressionable
homeschooled Christian children:

paper losses and gains
in estimation

from across backyards,
installation of logpiles and Camaro

bucket seats, rack of rakes:
unregistered pickup trucks

and registered pickup trucks:
birthright's systemic amplitude,

daughters longing for the long-gone:
an Econoline to hold winter

clothes or commune with former
owners, rusting cenotaph to all

the Poughkeepsie dead
lost to park-bench habit

III.

We speak to remind ourselves
of the far-flung fascination

with consuming bluntness
or checks co-signed

off the to-do list: garbage
bags taut with winter

clothes and summer mildew,
and hand-sewn curtains

tint faces green
as an open chord

ringing until the furnace
ruins bare vision

through barer trees

IV.

The micromanagement
of sunlight and corrective bass

vibrations: an *n*th-
generation photocopy

returned to the glass
for another flash of light,

the kid who's never seen
a movie but still owns

a false conception of
the heartfelt, and stays

up later than anyone
else on his street: memory's

residue: monotony of
the too-small house, indexical

shadows moving along
wallpaper, the unequivocal

threshold: something
to soothe afternoon's

torn shroud, the gaps
between inner colloquies

and a radiator's fury

V.

We are always picked
up by a car at the edge
of the pedestrian mall:

bare bulb, ceiling
-hung, wire and wire
nuts from an old fixture,

untaped drywall,
sweatpants on doorknob,
futon on floor,

and we feel at home:
temporarily:

TWO PASTORALS (II)

White steeple, gold
cross, green
leaves lasting: radio
antenna and
bridge, barge
riverly northing,
nothing
and no one
but singular
soul's monologues
spit above salt
-etched cars, metered
gulls: stop signs
from indicating much
except this ossuary
of cigarette
ends and bottle
-caps beside a stoop
on the way in
-to the city:
black smoke blows

Under over
-blown cloud-cover
and tinfoil left
-overs: gravel
in brick, in
-nards of a Bic
pen but no ink
adequate to in
-scribe one last plan
-tain, four
-flowered, blooming
from a curb-crack

L'ENVOI

Je n'ai pas oublié, voisine de la ville,
Notre blanche maison, petite mais
tranquille;

—Charles Baudelaire,
Les Fleurs du Mal

The blurriest clouds
of rosy-gray midnight

seen from clover
-leaf on-ramp across dirt

-piled scrapings, trajectories
of reverence for

dicey escapism spot
-lit by precise

sodium-arc auras:
and when I ask you

to lie down it does
not mean forever dead

-ended against
a security gate

Notes

In "The Poughkeepsiad," the phrase "we find ourselves plagued by unimaginable / circumstances" is taken from the statement issued by the family of Kendall Francois after his arrest for killing eight women in Poughkeepsie between 1996 and 1998 and hiding their bodies in his family's home; the line "My life now is very economical" is taken from Michael Palmer's poem "Notes for Echo Lake 4."

In "[The greatest poverty is not to live]," the line "The greatest poverty is not to live / in" is taken from Wallace Stevens's poem "Esthétique du Mal." In "[The elegance of an only focus, a trance]," the line "a form / of beauty nobody realized was beautiful" is taken from a 1981 interview with Virgin Prunes, published in *Vinyl* magazine. "[The absent tenant's electricity...]" makes reference to Charles Baudelaire's poem "Windows."

In "Hooker Avenue Serenade," the line "I'm like / the king of a rainy country" is taken from Charles Baudelaire's poem "Spleen (III)," as translated by Richard Howard.